THE STUDIO

THE STVDIO LTD.
A FAMILY AFFAIR.

RUTH ARTMONSKY

FRONT COVER Illustration Aubrey Beardsley for the first issue of *The Studio*.
INSIDE COVERS AND ENDPAPERS Original advertisments from *The Studio*, June 1912.
TITLE PAGE Covers of *The Studio Yearbook of Decorative Art*, 1906; *Art & Industry* magazine, July 1950; *The Studio*, September 1948 and *Modern Publicity*, 1932.
BACK COVER *The Studio* monogram, 1920s.

ACKNOWLEDGEMENTS

My thanks to Stella Harpley and Eduardo Sant'Anna for their help with the illustrations and my gratitude to James and Brian Webb for their enthusiasm and masterly design.

THE STUDIO LTD.
A FAMILY AFFAIR

Published by Artmonsky Arts
ISBN 978-1-7385016-1-8

Flat 1, 27 Henrietta Street
London WC2E 8NA
Telephone: 020 7240 8774
Email: artmonskyruth@gmail.com
www.ruthartmonsky.com

Text © Ruth Artmonsky 2024

Every effort has been made to trace the copyright holders and obtain permission to reproduce this material. Please contact the publisher with any enquiries relating to images or the rights holders.

Designed by Webb & Webb Design Limited
www.webbandwebb.co.uk

Printed in Great Britain

CONTENTS

7 INTRODUCTION

THE PLAYERS

11 *The Family*

25 *The Mainstay*

27 *The Bit-players*

33 *THE STUDIO* AND *THE STUDIO* SPECIALS

49 *THE STUDIO YEARBOOK OF DECORATIVE ART*

59 *COMMERCIAL ART* AND *MODERN PUBLICITY*

75 *HOW TO DO IT* AND OTHER SERIES

81 EPILOGUE

INTRODUCTION

The founding of The Studio Ltd., was fuelled by a mission – the idea that if countries learned about the cultures of other countries through visuals, rather than language, there would be better understanding, and resulting harmony. Charles Holme, retired from his career of trading across the Far East, and, with this charming, but naïve, notion in mind, aided by the capital he had accumulated, was able to set up a publishing business to launch an art magazine intent to draw its features and illustrations from across the world.

The Studio Ltd. started life in Covent Garden, in Henrietta Street, but soon settled into 44 Leicester Square, where it was to remain for some forty years until bombed out in the Blitz, whereon it moved back across the Charing Cross Road to Chandos Place.

The first issue of *The Studio* magazine was in 1893, and with this under his belt, Charles got the publishing bug. Not long afterwards, he put out an associated annual, *The Studio Yearbook of Decorative Art* and, what he termed Studio 'Specials', books on art and artefacts not adequately covered in his magazine or annual.

When Charles's son Geoffrey took over the reins, on his father's retirement in 1919 (Charles died in 1923), he had already worked in the company for some years, and, sharing his father's interests in the arts, both 'fine' and 'applied', he rapidly expanded The Studio Ltd. both by building on his father's publications, and by acquisitions, extending its range to include commercial art, and, eventually, industrial design.

The bombing in November 1940 of 44 Leicester Square, offices of The Studio Ltd..

INTRODUCTION

In their turn, Geoffrey's sons, Rathbone and Bryan, joined the company. It was, perhaps, inevitable, that the missionary zeal of the founder was to get somewhat diluted over the generations, but, nevertheless, the grandsons were to play their parts, Rathbone in London and Bryan in New York, when an office was set up, launching the company's American offshoot, The Studio Publications Inc.

The Holme family, with appropriate help, was, for some sixty years, to steer The Studio Ltd through two world wars and the poor economic climes immediately after WWI, and in the late 1920s into the '30s. It was to become the largest publisher of books and magazines on art and design in Britain in the first half of the 20th century.

The aftermath of Geoffrey's unexpected death, in 1954, with consequential death duties, forced the sale of The Studio Ltd and its publications. Passed from one new owner to another, some of the publications had an extended life, but the company itself, as an entity, run by the Holme family, was at an end.

Although the company's records up to WWII were destroyed in the bombing, much of its history can be derived from its publications themselves, telling of the interests, attitudes and policy of the proprietors.

Frank Brangwyn (1867–1956)
poster for *The Studio*, 1899.

THE PLAYERS

CHARLES HOLME *GRANDFATHER/FOUNDER*

THE FAMILY

CHARLES HOLME
1848–1923

CHARLES GEOFFREY
1887–1954

THREE DAUGHTERS

RATHBONE
1911–1987

BRYAN
1913–1990

TWO DAUGHTERS

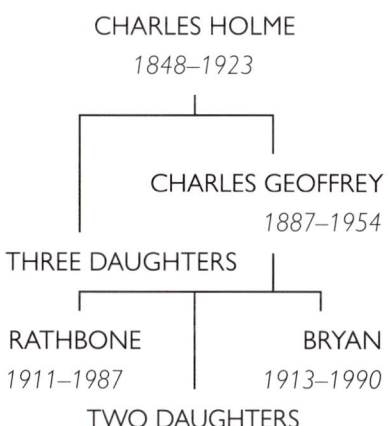

Charles Holme, portrait by Philip de László, 1908.

Although the journey from Derby, Charles' birthplace, and Bradford, where his father, a successful silk merchant, had sent the twenty year old to act as an agent to extend the family interests to wool, was less than a hundred miles, an odd occurrence in Bradford was to send him much further afield, some thousands of miles, to the Far East.

Not disinterested in profit, Charles Holme was ever more motivated by interest, by what caught his imagination. It is recorded that while resident in Bradford, Charles attended a lecture, in 1873, at the Bradford Chamber of Commerce, by a traveller recently returned from Turkestan. Within a year Charles, inspired, had set up The Central Asia Trading Company, to import goods such as carpets, embroideries, and such like, from Turkestan, India and China, while exporting to these lands Bradford woollens. Although the company only survived some five years it was to motivate Charles' pioneer trading across Asia.

This was not only to be a commercial challenge, dealing with suspicious natives, but, at times, a physical one, as when skirting the Himalayas. Nothing daunted, Charles was to extend his interests from Turkestan, India and China to Japan, not infrequently resorting to bartering, when such items as British sewing machines would be exchanged for decorative artefacts; these he began to collect for himself as well as to trade, and were to become a passion.

THE STUDIO LTD.

It is not recorded how Charles met Christopher Dresser, the designer, and came to set up a partnership with him, but it was presumably through their mutual enthusiasm for things Japanese. Throughout the last decades of the nineteenth century, after Japan had opened up its ports in 1854, Europe became awash with the cult of Japanism – Japanese pavilions started to appear in international exhibitions, European 'fine' artists began to be influenced by Japanese woodcuts, and retailers, such as Samuel Bing in Paris, were to build their reputations on specializing in Japanese artefacts. Dresser was a major crusader in the cult, having been invited to visit Japan by the British government. In 1882, he wrote of the impressions he had gained over some four months, one of the first books on Japanese culture – *Japan, its Architecture, Art and Art-manufacturers* published in 1882, which was to receive academic acclaim.

In 1879 Charles and Dresser entered into a partnership, Dresser & Holme, setting up an emporium in Farringdon Road – 'Oriental Merchants'. Dresser had been accompanied on his visit to Japan by two of his sons, Louis and Christopher, who were to arrange the import of the goods that were to become a major feature of the store. *The Furniture Gazette* wrote of it –

From the moment we entered we seem to have left England and to have been transported to Japan.

Christopher Dresser wallpaper design featured in *The Studio*, November 1898.

Dresser was to withdraw from the partnership in 1882 on the grounds of ill-health, and, for a time, Charles ran it on his own, eventually selling it in 1889.

Dresser & Holme were shareholders in and suppliers of goods to the Art Furnishers Alliance, which had a store in New Bond Street, established in 1880. Arthur Lasenby Liberty was a fellow shareholder and a known Japanese devotee, having started his career in the Oriental Department of Farmer & Rogers in Regent Street before setting up his own emporium across the road. Dresser and Liberty were close, and Charles, in his turn, became both a dealer for, and a friend of Liberty. Their relationship was such that Liberty virtually gave Charles carte blanche to import what goods he would for the brand new Liberty store.

Charles and his wife Clara became close friends with the Libertys, visiting each other and travelling abroad together. In 1888–89 the two couples, along with the painter Alfred East, made an eight month tour, taking in Egypt, Ceylon, Hong Kong, and Japan, returning home via America and Canada. East had been commissioned by the Fine Art Society to spend six months in Japan, producing some hundred works which were later exhibited in the Society's gallery. Charles wrote up their travels in a book, for which Liberty's wife, Emma supplied the photographs. Such was their shared enthusiasm, that Charles and Liberty were in at the founding of the Japan Society –

for the encouragement of Japanese studies and
for bringing together all those in the United Kingdom
and throughout the world interested in Japanese matters.

Photograph from *Japan. A pictorial record by Mrs. Lasenby Liberty*, 1899.

THE STUDIO LTD.

Charles was to become the Society's Vice-President and was rewarded, in 1902, with the Order of the Rising Sun.

It was from the difficulties Charles had found in his various dealings with different cultures, that he developed his notion that language was a major barrier to inter-cultural understanding, and that if countries could just see the cultural histories of others they would come to appreciate them and international harmony would exist. This became so strong an incentive that, as has been noted, Charles, still only in his early forties, stood aside from his trading activities in 1892, and, by the very next year, The Studio Ltd. had come into being, and the first issue of *The Studio* magazine was on the market, with its intention of illustrating cultures across the continents.

Charles' enthusiasm masked a limited knowledge and understanding of contemporary 'fine' art, and no experience at all of publishing, journalism or editing. In setting up and running The Studio Ltd. Charles was giving himself a kind of apprenticeship – he developed himself into a publisher and editor, albeit ever something of an amateur.

Matters Japanese were to filter into many of the early copies of *The Studio*, the odd article written by Charles himself, along with him penning four The Studio 'Specials', on Japanese landscapes, figures, birds and geishas. And many of the advertisements carried by the magazine were from importers of Japanese goods, as George Mackay of New Street, Birmingham 'important to collectors of Japanese art objects', and Murdoch & Co. 'importers of Japanese art albums'. Readers were aware, from the start, that *The Studio* was to be an international magazine.

Red House, Bexleyheath, London, commissioned by William Morris as a family home in 1859.

The aesthetic enthusiasms, which guided Charles in the way he developed The Studio Ltd., were equally strong in his home life. For some fourteen years (1889–1903) the family owned Philip Webbs' Red House, in Bexleyheath, that he had designed for William Morris. There have been attempts to link Charles to the Morris tradition as both were interested in pre-industrial crafts, but their furnishing of the house could not have been more different – Morris had a few pieces of beautifully designed furniture arranged scantily across the rooms, 'simplification' being key, whilst Charles was an extreme example of Victorian cramming, not a niche left unfilled. He did not seem at all daunted by the Morris legend, doing his own thing, but luckily did not interfere with the actual house structure itself. A further attempt has been made to suggest that Charles started the house becoming a place of pilgrimage, as once belonging to Morris. It is true that there was a constant stream of visitors when Charles was in residence, but many of these were Japanese dignitaries, come to discuss common interests and to see his extraordinary collection with little interest in the Morris connection.

In 1903 Charles bought The Old Manor House at Upton Grey, in Hampshire, parts of which were said to be from the fifteenth century. This Charles had altered by Ernest Newton (to be President of the Royal Institute of British Architects); yet again Charles collection of Oriental objets d'art crammed into the house, along with Georgian furniture, pre-Raphaelite paintings, books on art, and bonsai trees.

THE STUDIO LTD.

But along with the house came land, and if Charles were not to be remembered for founding The Studio Ltd., he is still considered a person of note, marked out for commissioning Gertrude Jekyll, by then well into her sixties, to design what is considered to be one of her most beautiful wild gardens, along with a kitchen garden, an orchard and more. Charles' interest, knowledge and strong opinions on gardens, led him to publish three Specials, between 1907 and 1911, on gardens across the South West, the Midland and Eastern, and Northern Counties of England.

Charles, not only founded The Studio Ltd. but built its reputation through its monthly magazine *The Studio*, its annual *The Studio Annual of Decorative Arts* and the *The Studio*s spin-offs, its Special books and 'series'; it was Charles' son, Geoffrey, who was to build the company into its domination of its genre in the publishing industry. Charles' three daughters are not reported as having been proffered, nor themselves offering, to contribute to the family company in any capacity.

CHARLES GEOFFREY HOLME SON/EXPANSIONIST

Charles was fortunate to have a son who, although not perhaps going so far as to aim for international harmony, shared his interests when it came to art and design and the desire to help, to educate, others to a similar appreciation.

Charles Geoffrey Holme, using C.G. Holme, C. Geoffrey Holme, or just Geoffrey Holme, to avoid confusion with his father, was born in Hampstead and educated at Abbotsholme. He is recorded as spending sometime

Geoffrey Holme, c.1918.

traveling, (a mini-20th century grand tour), before serving in WWI, initially with the Royal Army Service Corps in France, and then with GHQ Home Forces.

Seemingly without any specifically related prior training, Geoffrey was to join the family firm, taking over full responsibility on his father's retirement in 1919. He rose brilliantly to the task, not only editing *The Studio*, but its annual on decorative art, and the majority of *The Studio*'s Specials. Not content with this, Geoffrey was to broaden the reach of the company by buying an existing journal *Commercial Art* and, after some trialling, establishing an associated annual *Modern Publicity* – bringing advertising, publicity, and eventually industrial design within the company's gamut, but modestly, and appropriately, leaving their editing to someone else.

When it came to 'fine' art, Geoffrey seems to have taken a middle path, being adamantly against 'wild self-expression'. He was to write three articles for The Studio titled 'What is Modern Art', expressing this stand, later to be published as a book. Typical of his stance was his challenging of Barbara Hepworth and Ben Nicholson, in interview – 'What is the use of your art?'.

Although occasionally Geoffrey gave a nod to his father's passion for things Japanese, including the odd article on the subject in one or other of the firm's publications, and writing some four books, around 1930, on *Glories of Old Japan from Japanese Colour Prints*, his own passion was for photography. Charles, had not ignored the subject, publishing a Special in 1905,

The Golden Horn, Constantinople (now Istanbul, Turkey), photograph by Charles Geoffrey Holme.

Art in Photography, in which examples were drawn from both Europe and America, but Geoffrey was to fully indulge himself in his passion. He was to launch an annual on the subject – *Modern Photography* – in 1931, which ran for some twelve years, himself as editor; wrote several articles on photography for *The Studio*, (some including his own photographs); produced a Special in 1932 – *Touring the Ancient World with a Camera*; and edited Walter Nurnberg's *Special Photography in Commerce*, around 1940.

And if Geoffrey were not busy enough in his work, his leisure was equally filled with his passions. His son Bryan wrote of his father – 'I never saw my father but that he was engaged in something practical', such, included painting, constructing things and gardening. And additionally Geoffrey was involved in art and design affairs beyond work and home. He served on the Council of the Royal Society of Arts, on exhibition committees, experimented with pottery with his friends the Wedgwoods, and worked alongside the American Raymond Loewy when he was revamping the Lyons Corner House Company. For Geoffrey, whilst leaning towards the traditional when it came to 'fine' art, was to get swept up with enthusiasm for industrial design, the latest design area at the time to be gaining professional status. He was to sit on the Government Committee on Industrial Design, and, in 1934, wrote a Special – *Industrial Design and the Future*, one of the earliest books on the subject to be published in Britain. If Geoffrey were to be briefly characterised it must be as both passionate and energetic!

Geoffrey, as his father, was to purchase an old house, half Queen Anne, half Georgian, in the country, at Rivenhall in Essex. He had inherited much of his father's collection and did not hold back from adding to it from his own interests. He began to semi-retire in the late 1930s into the 1940s, delegating increasingly to his sons and work colleagues. For a time he lived with his younger son Bryan, who had become an American citizen, and was to die, in 1954, on a family holiday in Mexico.

Geoffrey once said 'art book publishing is the easiest way to loose one's shirt'; but it was only with his death that the company became topless in more than one way.

RATHBONE & BRYAN *GRANDSONS/INHERITORS*

Both Geoffrey's sons were educated at Oundle, and joined the family firm straight from school, without any further full-time education. Rathbone (known to his friends as Robin), the elder by two years, is said to have joined the editorial side of the business in 1928. Bryan was to describe Rathbone's role in London as making a major contribution, but he is not recorded specifically as editing any publication until 1941, presumably acting as assistant to his father till then. For *The Studio*, in 1941, he was titled 'acting' editor. It was after that, from the late 1940s through the 1950s, that he took on the co-editorship, along with Kathleen Frost, of the *Yearbook of Decorative Art*. It is possible that Rathbone found the editorial side of the company something of a challenge, for later he would describe himself as 'desk-bound', with few excursions

Industrial Design and the Future, Geoffrey Holme, published by The Studio, London 1934.

out, comparing his lot unfavourably to the immense amount of travelling that had been done, and enjoyed, by his father and grand-father.

However, Rathbone had shown artistic talent at school, having been fortunate enough to have been taught by E. M. O'Rorke Dickey (later to distinguish himself as educationalist, academic and administrator). And Rathbone's artistic interest seems to have continued after he had joined the firm, his spending a short time at the American printer's William Edwin Rudge, studying typography and lay-out. This would appear to have paid off, for later, after 1945, besides his editorial responsibilities, he is mentioned as Art Director for all the firm's publications. That Rathbone saw nothing demeaning in artists using their talents commercially is perhaps hinted at in a rare occurrence of his actually contributing an article to *The Studio* (on Frank Wootton, the artist of aircraft) –

> Unless an artist is self-disciplined to a remarkable degree – an artist, that is, who paints what he wants because he wants – he is unlikely to enjoy the advantages of as wide an experience as the commercial artist, who must be able to embrace almost every form of subject matter within his repertoire.

This 'wide experience' Rathbone would certainly have found, given the variety of the company's publications. Like his father, Rathbone's aesthetic preferences seem to have been relatively 'middle of the road'; examples of

Charles' grandsons, Rathbone and Bryan Holme.

his own style of painting certainly support this. He was to write of 'contemporary' experiments –

Linen Flowers, Rathbone Holme.

One may not be in sympathy with current trends in the visual arts, preferring perhaps the aesthetic appeal of a Japanese camera to a piece of derelict plumbing mounted on a pedestal.

Reflecting on the thirty or so years he was involved with The Studio Ltd. Rathbone described what was going on, presumably including his own contribution, as 'dedicated amateurism', employers and employees putting their hands to whatever was necessary at the time, without specialized training.

Bryan, however, appears to have had both verbal and commercial strengths to offer, along with, perhaps, a more sidelined appreciation of the arts than either his brother or his father, both of whom enjoyed painting. He wrote of his early years with the company as a kind of haphazard apprenticeship – with periods wrapping *The Studio* for dispatch; then delivering it; then trying to sell it to bookshops around the Charing Cross Road; actually invoicing for it; and, finally, undertaking the arduous task of trying to sell advertising space in the monthly.

Although both arduous, and sometimes boring, all of this would have proved useful when his father sent him, along with the company's commercial manager, Frank Mercer, and with secretarial support from Kathleen Frost, at the tender age of twenty-one, to New York, to establish an office there to sell the company's publications across America. This proved something of a challenge, not only because of his youth, but because much of what was being published by The Studio Ltd had a focus that was altogether more attractive to the European market than to that of the United States. Bryan was later to claim that it was only when the company hit upon appealing to the amateur artist and designer, with its more technical 'How To Do It' series, that the American offshoot survived at all in its early years.

Most of the activities of the New York office were initially London-led, but gradually Bryan seems to have built up the necessary experience and confidence to begin suggesting possible titles for publication, to provide an 'American Commentary' (sending news items over for inclusion in *The Studio*), to edit some publications, and even to begin to write books on the arts himself, as with a Studio Special in 1941 – *Book of Animals*, and with the company's American publishing title The Studio Publications Inc., when in 1944, he collaborated with Marcel Vertes for the book *Art & Fashion*.

Bryan, titled the President of The Studio Publications Inc., was to spend the rest of his career in America, becoming so assimilated as to have *The New York Times*, in its obituary of him, describe him as an American author. After his years with the company, books were to flood from his pen, through the 1960s, right up to his death in 1990, mostly written on subjects allied in some way to the arts.

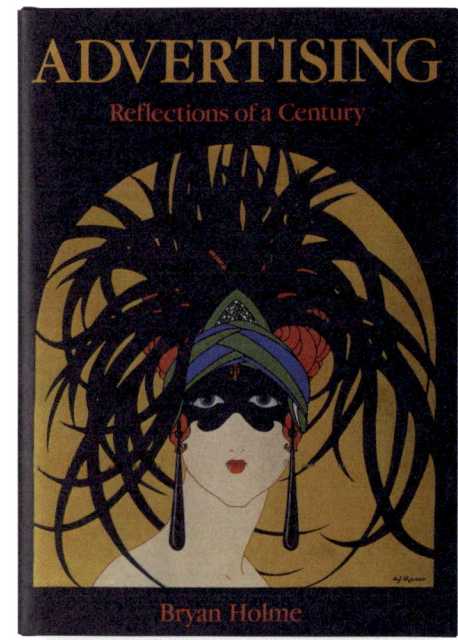

Cover of *Advertising: Reflections of a Century*, Bryan Holme, The Viking Press, 1982.

THE PLAYERS

FRANK A. MERCER (1889–1966) *THE MAINSTAY*

Portrait of Frank Mercer, pastel by Eric Kennington, 1943.

In 1959 Frank A. Mercer was awarded the Royal Society of Arts Bicentenary Medal for his influence in promoting art and design in British industry. It is understandable that the RSA made much of him for he had been a Council member for some seventeen years, had sat on various of its design-related committees (as the one nominating people to become Royal Designers of Industry), had advised on the design of the Society's newsletter, and had been its Treasurer for some five years. In awarding Mercer the medal he was described as having 'unsurpassed knowledge of international developments of advertising', and as having 'liveliness of eye and imagination'.

The name Holme so dominated The Studio Ltd. publications in the readership's eye, that Mercer's was rather overlooked. Yet it was Mercer, largely single-handedly, who edited the annual *Modern Publicity* throughout its existence, and, with co-editors, the monthly *Commercial Art/Art & Industry*; his name still appearing in an editorial role even after it was sold. Advertising, publicity and industrial design became his terrain, although he was also to intrude, occasionally, on what was largely Holme territory – editing both series of *Gardens and Gardening* in the 1930s and '50s, and several of the Specials (including *Royal London* and *Royal Palaces* in 1935, and *Poster Progress* in 1939).

On Mercer's reception of the RSA medal, Robert Downer, then editor under its new ownership of the re-jigged *Art & Industry – Design in Industry*, wrote of Mercer's years of editing that he was –

THE STUDIO LTD.

…responsible for shaping and enlargening the editorial policy of this publishing house for more than thirty years…He exercised a steady influence on the progress of good design in all departments of industry.

It was Mercer, in his editorial role, who helped make commercial artists respectable, and to build commercial art as a profession; and it was Mercer who stirred British industry to catch up with the Americans lead in industrial design. He could be said to have had a reputation for that alone, but it was he, with what Bryan termed 'astuteness', that became the mainstay of The Studio Ltd. when it came to its profitability.

Little is recorded of Mercer's career before he joined The Studio Ltd in 1919. There are hints that he had undergone some art training before serving in WWI, which is where he and Geoffrey got to know each other. He was appointed to the company initially as commercial manager, but such must have been his effectiveness, that it was he who was dispatched to America in 1932 (along with the young green Bryan and the elusive Miss Kathleen Frost) to set up the New York office, becoming its first President in the years running up to WWII, supervising its operation. And such must have been his contribution in London, that from Managing Editor he was to advance to Managing Director and eventually Chairman of the company.

'Book Row', Fourth Avenue, New York, 1940s, the location of The Studio Ltd.'s New York office.

THE BIT-PLAYERS

The actual first editor of The Studio Ltd.'s first publication *The Studio* was Joseph Gleeson White, who was brought in by default when C. Lewis Hind, who had done the dummy of a possible art magazine which Charles was to run with, was tempted away by a better offer from William Waldorf Astor. Gleeson White, the last minute fallback, was an established art journalist at George Bell & Sons, to whom Charles must have been grateful, not himself having any experience of either publishing or editing. His gratitude appears to have been expressed in indulging Gleeson White by letting him write some of the earliest *The Studio* Specials on his pet subjects – Christmas cards, children's illustrated books and book-plates – none of which were likely to be best-sellers. Gleeson White not only must have been a guide for Charles, but was to establish much of what was to be *The Studio* content and layout, as well as deciding that it should be photo-mechanically printed.

Although in chronological pecking order William Gaunt was not the first to share editorship, if he comes within the category 'bit-player' at all, he certainly was primus inter pares, on the grounds of long service, let alone quality of contribution. It has always been assumed that the W.S. Gaunt, who worked alongside Mercer editing *Commercial Art/Art & Industry* and *Modern Publicity*, was the self-same William Gaunt, 'fine' artist and academic art historian. Although some have wondered at his dirtying his hands with such commercial art activities as advertising and publicity, such doubts

Joseph Gleeson White by Frederick Hollyer, 1897.

can perhaps be allayed by the surfacing, in a sale in a London art gallery in 1931, of a pencil and water colour by the artist William Gaunt, entitled 'The Advertising Exhibition', a rare subject for a 'fine' artist, ridiculing the industry that was to provide his bread-and-butter for so many years.

Gaunt not only acted as co-editor of the company's publications on commercial art but provided the text for a number of its Specials, from *Rome Past and Present* in 1926, to *Bandits in a Landscape*, a study of romantic painting from Caravaggio to Delacroix in 1937. That Geoffrey particularly valued Gaunt is perhaps illustrated by his inviting him to provide the text for a Special of Geoffreys' photographs – *Touring the Ancient World with a Camera*, published in 1932.

Other co-editors, minnows when compared with Gaunt, in that they flitted on to the stage for rather brief performances, were Shirley B. Wainwright who worked with Geoffrey on a number of issues of *The Studio Annual of the Decorative Arts* in the 1930s, Grace Lovat Fraser, who co-edited with Mercer *Art & Industry* at the beginning of WWII, and Charles Rosner who co-edited with Mercer some editions of *Modern Publicity* in the immediate post-war years.

Geoffrey could well have come to regret the involvement of Shirley B. Wainwright in decorative art concerns. He had invited Wainwright to provide an introduction for the 1923 issue, of *The Yearbook of Decorative Arts*, perhaps feeling unsure of his own competence to write on such matters as interior design. Not only did Wainwright hog the first eight pages of that annual, but managed to slip in a number of illustrations of his own work as

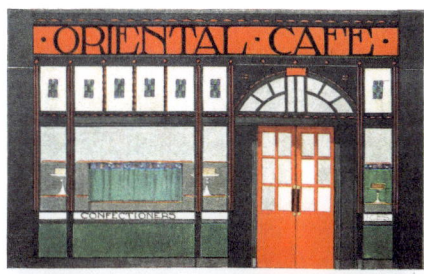

OPPOSITE *The Advertising Exhibition*, William Gaunt, 1931.

ABOVE Shop fronts designed by Shirley B. Wainwright, 1921.

furniture designer and interior decorator. And this sleight of hand, as it were, was to follow in the next few issues, through to 1930 – of assistance to Geoffrey, but gaining free publicity for himself.

Grace Lovat Fraser, helping out at the start of WWII with the editing of *Art & Industry*, (Gaunt being involved with producing paintings for the war artists' committee), was referred to as 'associate' editor. She was not only to act in this role but to provide several articles for the monthly, including its first major one on the publicity work of the new Ministry of Information, with further ones on the allied work of the Ministry of Food and the Cotton Board. Generally dismissed as merely the wife of the designer Claude Lovat Fraser, Grace was a force in her own right – setting up a design firm with Norman Wilkinson after her husband's premature death, working in the design departments of Schweppes and Venesta, and serving, for a time in the Research and Industrial Design Departments of the advertising agency Pritchard, Wood & Partners. At the time she was helping Mercer out she also wrote a Special – *Doll Making at Home*.

In the December 1941 issue of *Art & Industry* Mercer announced Grace's departure on 'an important mission to the United States, which will take her from coast to coast'; and that she is to be admired for her courage and enterprise in undertaking this. America was yet to join the Allies and there was a good deal of activity both in commercial art and industrial design for her to survey. Mercer suggested that some of her findings would be fed back to the magazine's readers, but if this did take place it wasn't featured as such.

Grace Lovat Fraser photographed in London, 1915.

THE PLAYERS

Charles Rosner, born in Budapest, had already acted as Hungarian correspondent for The Studio Ltd. from the early 1930s. He came to live in England in 1939, becoming naturalised in 1947. He was to build a reputation as an art critic and became associated both with the Sylvan Press and with *Graphis*.

And then there was the elusive Kathleen Frost, who came to co-edit, with Rathbone, in the late 1940s and into the 1950s, both for *Decorative Art*, and for a Special – *Modern Lettering and Calligraphy* in 1954. As late as 1955, Mercer is thanking her for her help with the 1955/6 issue of *Modern Publicity* –

Special acknowledgement is due to Miss Kathleen Frost who, incidentally, was the first sub-editor of *Art & Industry*, for stepping into the breach at such short notice and sub-editing this volume.

There seems to be a nuance between co-editing and sub-editing, the latter of a lesser status. Kathleen joined The Studio Ltd. in the 1930s, and was still there in the 1950s, and had been, in some capacity, essential to the trip that was to open up America. It is only by chance, easily to be missed, that readers learned, when a photograph of her appeared in an issue of *The Studio*, along with photographs of Rathbone and Bryan, that she was a secretary, albeit the leading one for over twenty years, the one the company seems to have looked to for special support when emergences or challenges arose.

K.M. (Kathleen) Frost, secretary of The Studio Ltd. from 1929.

31

FIRST PART OF A NEW VOLUME

THE · STUDIO

An Illustrated Magazine of Fine & Applied Art

OCT. 16 '95

VOL. 6 No. 31

THE SUPPLE-
MENTAL ILLUS-
TRATIONS WITH
THIS NUMBER
ARE BY AUBREY
BEARDSLEY
KATE LIGHT
AND MORIKAWA
SOBUN

5 Henrietta Street
Covent Garden
LONDON W.C

Monthly
1/-

THE STUDIO &
THE STUDIO SPECIALS

In 1968, *Studio International*, claiming to be of direct descent of *The Studio* brought out a special issue celebrating *75 Years of The Studio*. As to be expected it overflowed with praise from the great and the good along the lines of Herbert Read's contribution –

any adequate history of the modern movement
in art will have to take account of the significant
part played by *The Studio*.

The less obsequious Kenneth Clark and Victor Pasmore threw doubts on such a claim; Clark wrote –

Not all the works of art produced in *The Studio* were
equally distinguished; much of the painting was mediocre
and the applied design was painfully artistic.

And Pasmore went even further, recalling how, for him, *The Studio* faded into insignificance when he arrived in London and became aware of what actually was avant garde. *The Studio* throughout its existence, and, in retrospect, was to attract both fans and detractors.

The cover of an early issue of *The Studio* magazine from Henrietta Street, October, 1895.

THE STUDIO.

EDITED BY CHARLES HOLME.

Contents, October 16th, 1895.

LOOSE SUPPLEMENT.—"ISOLDE," A DRAWING IN FOUR COLOURS BY AUBREY BEARDSLEY.

	PAGE
THE HERKOMER SCHOOL. By A. LYS BALDRY. Twelve Illustrations	3
AN AMERICAN SCULPTOR: FREDERICK MACMONNIES. By ROYAL CORTISSOZ. Five Illustrations	17
FRENCH WOODWORK AT SOUTH KENSINGTON. By E. F. STRANGE. Nine Illustrations	26
AN ARTISTIC TREATMENT OF COTTAGES. By HORACE TOWNSEND. Ten Illustrations	29
THE BAG OF THE BEE. A Poem Illustrated by KATE LIGHT	35
EGYPT AS A SKETCHING GROUND. By PERCY BUCKMAN. Seven Illustrations	37
THE NATIONAL COMPETITION. Eighteen Illustrations	42
A SERIES OF JAPANESE DRAWINGS—I. BIRD AND BRANCH. By MORIKAWA SOBUN	50
STUDIO-TALK. (From Our Own Correspondents)—	
LONDON . . . 53 PARIS . . . 55	
GLASGOW . . . 53 BRUSSELS . . . 55	
BIRMINGHAM . . 54 BERLIN . . . 56	
NEWLYN . . . 54 DRESDEN . . . 57	
NEW PUBLICATIONS. Two Illustrations	58
AWARDS IN OUR PRIZE COMPETITIONS. Fifteen Illustrations	61
THE LAY FIGURE AT HOME	68

NOTICE TO CONTRIBUTORS.

The Editor of THE STUDIO cannot hold himself responsible in any case for the return of Articles or Sketches. He will, however, always be glad to consider any suitable Manuscripts or Drawings which may be submitted to him, and will make every effort to return those not accepted, provided postage stamps are enclosed at the time they are sent.

All Contributions should be addressed, "The Editor," Offices of THE STUDIO, 5 Henrietta Street, Covent Garden, London, W.C.

STUDIOS, ETC., TO BE LET AND WANTED.

The Proprietor is prepared to insert small prepaid Advertisements in THE STUDIO, at a minimum charge of Five Shillings for thirty words (four lines). Orders, accompanied by Stamps or Postal Orders, to reach the Advertisement Manager at the Office of THE STUDIO, 5 Henrietta Street, Covent Garden, W.C., not later than the 5th of each month.

A. KNAPP & CO.,
26 SAVILE ROW, REGENT ST.
(*Facing New Burlington St., W.*)

JAPANESE CURIOS, WORKS OF ART, &c.

Netsukes.	Some very fine Specimens of Modern Work in Lacquer, &c.	Lac Boxes.
Tsubas.		Bronzes.
Inroes.		Cloisonne.

SECOND-HAND DIAMOND JEWELLERY,
PRECIOUS STONES, &c.
JEWELLERY REPAIRED AND MOUNTED.

Established 1878.   *Inspection Invited.*

CRAMER & CO.   **PIANOS BY ALL MAKERS.** THE LARGEST ASSORTED STOCK OF PIANOS in London. Instruments by all the good makers MAY BE SEEN AND COMPARED. BEST CASH PRICES, or on CRAMER'S INSTALMENT SYSTEM.

CRAMER & Co.'s Celebrated PIANOS from £24 net. Large Stock of SECOND-HAND INSTRUMENTS, from £15. Fully Illustrated Price Lists on application.

CRAMER & Co.'s MAGNIFICENT NEW PIANOFORTE GALLERY, "THE LARGEST IN EUROPE," 207 & 209 REGENT STREET, W.

IMPORTANT TO COLLECTORS OF JAPANESE ART OBJECTS.
GEORGE MACKEY, 74 NEW STREET, BIRMINGHAM,

Begs to call the attention of Collectors to his Large and Varied Stock of Japanese Goods, now in such request (including many fine examples recently purchased from well-known Private Collections), at prices to suit all classes of buyers.

1000 Netsuke	from 3s. to £3 each.	60 Swords and Daggers from 20s. to £10 each.
300 Inro	,, 10s. ,, £10 ,,	500 Fuchi Kashira . . . 10s. ,, £2 a pair.
400 Sword Guards	,, 5s. ,, £5 ,,	250 Kodzuka . . . 10s. ,, £2 each.

Ivory Carvings (Okimono) from 20s. to £20 each.

Wanted Postage Stamps of the greatest Value and Rarity only.

Several Fine Books of Original Drawings and Paintings (Japanese). Many very Rare and Fine Examples in Lac, Metal Work, Wood Carving, &c. Selections will be sent for inspection and approval on receipt of references. Japanese Collections Purchased. Visitors to Birmingham are cordially invited to inspect the Large Stock of Antique Furniture, China, Plate, Jewellery, Miniatures, Weapons, Enamels, Pictures, Engravings, &c. &c.

Just purchased a large Private Collection of all varieties of Japanese Art Objects, many of which were exhibited in the Burlington Fine Arts' Club last year. Also the entire Collection of Chinese and Japanese Articles known as "The TITSINGH Collection" from The Hague, Holland, wonderfully rich in old Porcelain and Pottery, Netsukes, Ivories, Lac, Bronzes and Books.

For the convenience of London Customers a Branch Shop has been opened by GEORGE MACKEY, at **No. 2 PALL MALL PLACE**, exactly opposite Messrs. Christie's Auction Rooms.

L. Cornelissen & Son, Artists' Colourmen.
SOLE AGENTS FOR THE UNITED KINGDOM FOR
DR. F. SCHOENFELD & CO.'S CELEBRATED OIL, WATER, GOUACHE COLOURS,
PETROLEUM COLOURS, AND TEMPERA COLOURS.

PAPERS FOR REPRODUCING ILLUSTRATIONS BY THE PHOTO-ZINCO PROCESSES.

PRICE LISTS ON APPLICATION.

22 GREAT QUEEN STREET, LONDON, W.C.

Although the founding of The Studio Ltd.'s first publication, *The Studio*, a monthly magazine, is generally attributed to Charles Holme, it, in fact, was the brainchild of one, C. Lewis Hind, a sub-editor of T*he Art Journal*. Keen to produce his own art magazine, Hind left his job in 1892, and produced a 'dummy', which he showed to his friend, the publisher, John Lane. One can only describe it as serendipity that Lane was also a friend of Charles, who, at about the same time, was also considering a magazine along much the same lines, but more international in character. In 1892 a contract was signed between Hind, art journalist, and Charles, the international businessman with funds.

At the last minute, Hind was tempted away by what he thought were surer prospects, working for the newspaper tycoon, William Waldorf Astor, Charles having to fall back on Gleeson White, as has been noted, as his first collaborating editor. Before he had departed Hind suggested to Charles that the magazine needed something sensational to launch its first issue, to feature something 'shocking'; Aubrey Beardsley was thought to fit the bill.

By 1895, Gleeson White too had departed, and Charles was left as sole proprietor of the company, sole editor of *The Studio*. He was to be completely in charge of operations through to his retirement in 1919. After that Geoffrey took over the baton, as it were, running the *The Studio*, through to his death. The family were to focus their interests on *The Studio* and its offshoots and leave the editing and publishing of the more earthy, commercial publications to Mercer and his co-operators.

The structure of the contents of *The Studio* was developed fairly early on – advertisements, articles, news (variously headed), exhibition dates and book

The back cover of an early issue of *The Studio* magazine from Henrietta Street, October, 1895. The 'Contents' relegated to the top left.

reviews. The layout was odd in more than one way; although the content had been displayed on the front cover for the early issues, later on it was tucked away in the top left hand corner of the back of the cover, lost amidst advertisements. Even when contents came to take up a whole page, it remained behind the cover – it was not to flaunt its wares again for some years. For the early issues, articles, comments, criticisms were all run together, so it was a challenge for the reader to sort out when one feature ended and another began. Although it had an eye-catching cover, the magazine's inner pages, for some years, left much to be desired when it came to typography and layout.

As was Charles' intent, *The Studio* displayed its internationalism from the start. Besides there actually being a French edition, in the early British issues were articles not only on places abroad that inspired British artists, but reports on contemporary and historical artworks from across the globe. Geoffrey kept a thread of internationalism going throughout his editorship, able to make much of what was on show at the Empire Exhibition at Wembley in 1924, and, after the American office had been established, examples from the whole of that continent, both north and south, areas that had not been so frequently sampled before.

What is often forgotten is that *The Studio* carried features on artefacts as well as on 'fine' art, often overlapping with what was the entire focus of *The Yearbook of Decorative Art*; articles on architecture, textiles, furnishing, jewellery and stage design. When it came to 'fine' art, on which its reputation was to be built, *The Studio* showed a curious restraint – what some critics have referred to as the magazine 'taking a middle way' – relatively little on the warring

THE STUDIO & THE STUDIO 'SPECIALS'

schisms of Fauvism, Cubism, Futurism, Surrealism, Abstract Expressionism and the like. If any of this was mentioned at all, it would tend to be found briefly in 'Notes', the section reporting on exhibitions currently being run in London and other capital cities.

Generally *The Studio* tended to avoid theoretical issues albeit Geoffrey did make one attempt, in 1932 issues of *The Studio* (later to be gathered into a Special book), to pen his views on 'modern' in 'fine' art, writing of what he considered wrong with it –

The painter must escape from modern theory…
abandon his natural sphere and pretend to a purism
and puritanism which has never been in the nature of
painters as long as the world has gone on.

He preferred the proper business of the painter to be 'the warm, breathing world of flesh and blood and living things'. One critic, thumbing through all the issues of *The Studio* in the 1930s, exploded on finding only one illustration of Henry Moore's work and that to do with interior design. Not only did Geoffrey seem not to care for abstraction or symbolism, but to dislike any form of excessive self-expression. He wrote of the self-indulgent artist –

ABOVE AND OPPOSITE Ben Nicholson abstracts, from *The Studio*, December 1945.

a doubt as to his genius never crosses his
mind, It never occurs to him to wonder if
the self he is expressing is particularly admirable.

THE STUDIO LTD.

ABOVE A typical 'pleasant' illustration; *Cliffs at Vaucottes*, oil painting by William Rothenstein, 1909.

OPPOSITE A 'challenging' illustration; *Heart of England; Homage to Richard Hillary*, pastel by Eric Kennington, c.1942-1944.

THE STUDIO LTD.

So the reader of *The Studio*, with Geoffrey as editor, got the pleasant, the technically admirable, but more rarely the disturbing or challenging. In the *Studio International* celebration issue of 1968, D.J. Gordon wrote –

a younger reader, brought up by the proper books to think of the early Studio as avant garde, herald of the Modern Movement, is apt to retire from it discomforted.

Another contributor, in similar mode, noted that they were almost shocked when they came across a poster for absinthe in its pages!

One has only to compare the rather staid output of *The Studio* under the Holmes with, say, its editorship by G.S. Whittet when it became to be owned by the Longacre Press (Odhams Press) in 1961, with an editorial on the warfare between the Royal Academy and the Fine Arts Committee, an article on art for investment, and illustration of the work of Jackson Pollock, Hans Hartung and Arthur Boyd.

Two early features in *The Studio* were included to encourage creativity. A Studio Competition was established, its competitors to be students and amateurs, the prizes generous – for some categories as much as three guineas, for many a week's wages. For each Competition there were a range of categories, not only for 'fine' art, but for 'applied' as 'Design for Industrial Purposes' and 'Design for Metalwork'.

And for further encouragement of students *The Studio* carried articles and illustrations demonstrating the kind of work the art schools

Another example of a 'challenging' illustration, *More Unpleasant People* by Pearl Binder.

THE STUDIO & THE STUDIO 'SPECIALS'

Examples of designs by Leeds School of Art students.

were producing, possibly to attract would be commissioners and potential employers. The features included both private and publicly funded schools across the country, no snobbery – the like of Stoke-on-Trent and Leeds, as well as posh Heatherlys and the well-reputed Regent Street Polytechnic. In 1916 Charles published a survey – 'Arts and Crafts, a review of the work executed by the students in the leading art schools of Great Britain'.

And when it came to encouraging amateurs further, the output of a hotchpotch of societies was brought to the eye of the reader, including the Civil Service Sketch Club and the English Wood Engraving Society. Although these efforts could be interpreted positively, as encouraging undeveloped talent, cynics would relate them rather to a concern to extend readership. The magazine came to overflow with hypes on young, unrecognised or under-rated artists, but the editors rarely seem to have backed a winner; few, now, would recognize the names of such as Violet Cornelli, Harry Morley or John Platt.

With no records in existence, it can only be a matter of surmise why, in the 1920s, The Studio Ltd. thought to buy an existing art journal – *Drawing and Design* (not long after it had brought the original *Commercial Art*); and, of even greater wonder letting loose one, Gerald Reitlinger, to edit it, a rare instance of when editorial responsibility lay outside the family or Mercer. Although the company only ran it for a few years (16 issues in all), Reitlinger showed what 'contemporary' was all about, warts and all. With some pomposity the first editorial declared –

THE STUDIO & THE STUDIO 'SPECIALS'

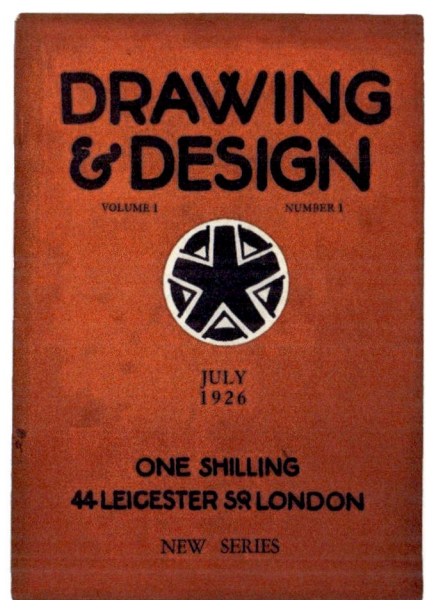

ABOVE The short-lived *Drawing & Design* journal, 1926.
OPPOSITE Clifford Webb, *Loading*, *The Studio* April 1932 (from the English Wood Engraving Society).

Its special function will be one which no other journal has assumed to any considerable extent- that of dealing with the methods and principles of art old and new in such a way as to establish a comparative standard of appreciation.

Perhaps the intent of the company was to supplement the content of *The Studio*, which rarely went deeply into anything dwelling on theory. With *Drawing and Design* the reader was going to be challenged to think. And as to artists featured, the reader got the likes of Frank Dobson, the Nash brothers and Matthew Smith rather than those in the style of Russell Flint. Reitlinger also claimed the first inclusion in an art magazine of film as an art. Politeness and restraint were out, argument in, along with a deluge of salacious nudism. Why did The Studio Ltd. sell it on in 1927? Was it becoming too controversial, or perhaps too crammed with the quirky preferences of its editor, or that, indeed, it became poorly edited with whole blocks of illustrations offered without rhyme or reason; all is surmise.

From its earliest years, in addition to *The Studio* magazine, the company began to publish *The Studio* Specials – books designed to cover subjects in depth that could only be dealt with superficially in the space available in its magazine. At first these were titled The Studio Specials, along with the season in which they were issued. They were to come out in all shapes and styles, some quite simply bound, others in tooled leather. Gradually the word

43

THE STUDIO LTD.

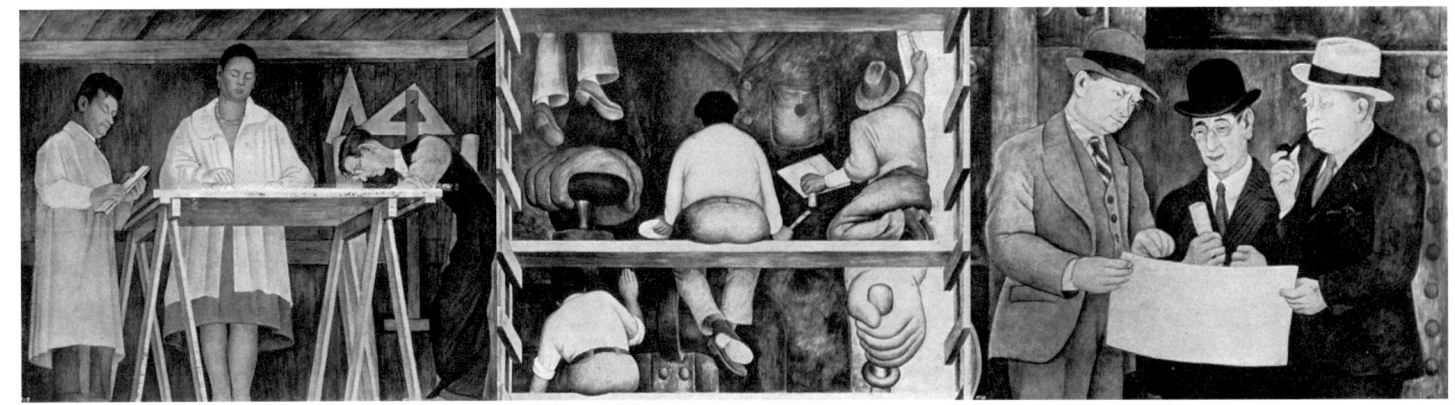

Frescos by Diego Rivera, 1932,
a less frequent example of
international work.

Lettering of today, 1941, cover design by Ashley Havinden.

season was dropped, and then the words *The Studio*; the Specials took on a life of their own and were to establish the company as a book publisher as well as a magazine one.

Although many of the Specials published in Charles' time were on English art, and historical at that (old houses, old mezzotints, old colour prints, and such), he seems to have kept true to his international intent with the odd Special on the culture of a specific country, such as Austria, and a whole run, that Geoffrey was to continue for a time, on peasant art in various European countries.

But Charles does seem to have made some effort, or, at least, to have allowed others, to use the Specials to record what was happening contemporarily, and the adjective 'modern' began to appear in the titles (*Modern Pen Drawing*, *Modern British Water-colours*, *Modern Etching*, and so on). With these, the company was not only introducing its readers to other cultures, but possibly felt able to be more adventurous; in *Lettering of Today*, first issued in 1937, readers would have been brought right up to date with examples from Barnett Freedman, Eric Gill, Milner Gray, McKnight Kauffer and Stanley Morrison; in *Contemporary Painting in Europe*, in 1939, readers would have been introduced to most of the European art movements and the works of the likes of Dali, Kandinsky, Derain, Grosz, Léger, Miró, Rouault and Segonzac.

Geoffrey was to tread much the same path as his father – many Specials on English art and artists, much of it historical, the odd one on the art of a specific country (as Spain, America, and USSR); and a few with the words 'modern' or 'contemporary' in their titles, daringly including such names as Kokoschka, Picasso, Braque, Cocteau, Rousseau and Rouault, rarely to be found in *The Studio* magazines of similar date. *Art in the USSR*, published in 1935, appears to have escaped the usual dignified appearance of the Specials, by flaunting a definitely constructivist cover. Two of the most 'contemporary' Specials, one that Geoffrey edited, the other, that he wrote, were *Modern Architecture* in 1929 (including the work of Le Corbusier, Walter Gropius and Frank Lloyd Wright); and *Industrial Design and the Future* for which Geoffrey supplied such examples as the Eastman Kodak Brownie camera, and Norman Bel Geddes' railway carriages and ocean liners.

When it came to British artists and designers Geoffrey was to prove rather more adventurous than his father in choice of subjects for Specials. For those on woodcuts and lithographs, included were Paul Nash, Eric Ravilious, Leon Underwood, Edward Wadsworth and C.R.W. Nevinson; for painters Laura Knight, Augustus John, Duncan Grant, Vanessa Bell and Stanley Spencer. As Geoffrey's confidence grew he seems to have become increasingly 'contemporary', yet still, it would seem, largely steering clear of the radical or controversial.

Over the years more than two hundred and fifty Specials were published, Charles editing many of them until his retirement, and Geoffrey until WWII; after that the family seem to have largely bowed out of editing Specials, with Rathbone and Bryan only associated with the odd one.

Art in the USSR, Charles Holme, The Studio Ltd., 1935.

ART
IN THE
USSR

DECORATIVE ART 1933

THE STUDIO YEAR BOOK

THE STUDIO YEAR BOOK OF DECORATIVE ART

The Studio Year Book of Decorative Art launched in 1906, (changing its name to *Decorative Art* in 1925), ran for over fifty years, only missing a few during the WWII and immediately after. The company's intent in publishing the annual was given in its first issue –

The Studio has month by month denoted a considerable portion of its space to applied art in its manifold forms… but the need of a more systematic and concentrated treatment has impressed the Editor with the desirability of preparing annually a volume in which it shall be treated throughout its entire range.

The editorship of the annual went down the family line, Charles to be followed by Geoffrey, who, in turn, was followed, for a short time, by Rathbone. Charles and Geoffrey seem to have largely edited for the annual on their own, but Geoffrey did bring in Shirley Wainwright for several years, in the 1920s, as has been noted. He had invited him to provide an Introduction for the 1923 issue, and, thereafter, until 1930, worked with him as co-editor. The readership were given no reason for Wainwright's arrival or departure, but, on surmise,

Decorative Art 1933 Yearbook.

THE STUDIO LTD.

it could have been that at the start Geoffrey was building up confidence to himself edit such a broad subject matter, and, for the departure, even a possible clash of personalities and style, for Wainwright seems to have been something of a publicist, encouraging a more self-congratulatory note than was Geoffrey's modest wont, as in the tone of the 1930 annual –

The Studio Yearbook has now existed for twenty-five years, and it has existed so long, and still flourishes, flourishes indeed, more than ever, because it has recognized not only the power but the profound meaning of Fashion. Its numbers from the very beginning have been devoted not to the ordinary house, but to the house that went one shade better, in whose design might be discerned the movement dictated by the general current of life; and in this way it has become a commentary and a supplementary volume to the social history of the first quarter of the century…

Although perhaps an exaggerated claim, there is an element of truth in it for the Annual did, in fact, demonstrate the result on design of such social changes as increased taxation of the wealthy, reducing patronage, shifting the market focus towards society's lower rungs with the inevitability of mass production; and along with such economic changes, came smaller dwellings, houses and flats with less floor space leading to the design of fitted and multi-purposed furniture; the reduction

Typical feature of an Edwardian edition – WM. Morris & Co. window designs.

of the employment of servants bringing with it increased need for labour saving devices; and so on; all this to be illustrated in the yearbook.

But, along with such considerations, the Yearbook, as Wainwright suggested, came to reflect fashion. With Charles as Editor, Arts & Crafts and Art Nouveau came and went, featuring the likes of Charles Ashbee, Charles Rennie Mackintosh, Edwin Lutyens, Liberty, Heals and such. And with Geoffrey came Art Deco, the Bauhaus etc. with illustrations of the designs of Le Corbusier, Walter Gropius, László Moholy-Nagy, and Serge Chermayeff; and, in the late 1930s, with the impact of industrial design, the Americans Walter Teague and Raymond Loewy. Post-war, when Rathbone edited, came the next generation of designers, including Ernest Race, Robin Day, Misha Black and the tsunami of Scandinavians. Unlike *The Studio* the Yearbook strained to be truly contemporary, up to the minute, if not a step ahead, as Wainwright had claimed.

A possible criterion of the Annual's success was the advertisements it attracted. Although most magazines (as compared to learned journals), needed advertising to survive financially, The Yearbook seems, at first, to have been reluctant to soil its hands with such, relying on the income from *The Studio* and its Specials, for it did not resort to including advertisements until Geoffrey's editorship, into the mid-1920s. Advertisers would only be likely to place their advertisements in publications where the readership was likely to be potential purchasers of their goods. Those choosing to advertise in the Yearbook were declaring

Photograph of *Maison Cook* designed by Le Corbusier, from a feature in *Decorative Art*, 1930s.

THE STUDIO LTD.

Featured in *Decorative Art* in the 1930s; Serge Chermayeff furniture for Waring & Gillow; Peter Jones tableware and the studio of Walter Dorwin Teague.

THE STUDIO YEAR BOOK OF DECORATIVE ART.

Advertisement for Kolster Brands in *Decorative Art*; 1930s.

positively that here was a journal contemporary in its content. Considering the advertisements in just one issue, that for 1934, the advertisers were validating the conversant, up-to-date, editorship, for there, at the back, were Gordon Russell, Marion Dorn, Wedgwood showing Keith Murray, Carter, Stabler & Adams showing Poole pottery, Bowman's, its furniture, and so on.. And this continued, into the 1950s when the Yearbook carried advertisements for the likes of Tibor Reich and David Whitehead's textiles, and Dunns of Bromley, along with the Scandinavians, Orrefors and Kosta Glass.

Nor did *Decorative Art* fail when it came to The Studio Ltd.'s intent to be international. Charles, with his total commitment to this, featured in early issues examples drawn from Europe, from Germany, Austria and Hungary; and went on to categorise illustrations by country of origin, including both European and further afield, as America and Canada, and, rarities of examples from South and East Africa. Geoffrey, more restless and experimental, tried out a variety of ways of demonstrating the Yearbooks internationalism, from having blocks of illustrations from various countries at the back of general sections as architecture, furniture and so on, to eventually mixing foreign examples with British ones, just indicating country of origin in the captions.

When it came to actual design of the Yearbook, editors never appear to have settled on a regular layout that readers could rely on, able immediately to turn to the sections that interested them most.

53

THE STUDIO LTD.

Advertisments from *Decorative Arts*, Gordon Russell, 1930s. From Liberty and The Design Centre in the 1950s.

THE STUDIO YEAR BOOK OF DECORATIVE ART.

Contents

Foreword: The Editors	6
American Architecture Today: Richard J. Neutra	7
Apartment in St John's Wood, London	13
House at Brentwood, California	14
House at Westhampton, Long Island, New York	15
House in West Vancouver, British Columbia	16
House in Pilar, Argentina	17
House in Tokyo	18
House in Vienna	19
Interiors and Furnishing	20
Kitchens and Bathrooms	48
Textiles	52
Wallpapers	66
Lighting	68
Glass	72
Ceramics	82
Tableware	96
Metalware	104
Decoration	114
Index	121

Typical 1950s contents page of *Decorative Art*.

Sometimes there would be an editorial, at other times not; and when one did appear it could be merely one page, or as long as an article over a number of pages. Sometimes, perhaps when a controversial matter was to be covered, the editor would ask a guest to write on what was occasionally headed 'Introduction'. The list of artists, designers and manufacturers whose work was being illustrated, along with advertisements, could sometimes be found at the front, sometimes at the back, with advertisements occasionally split between the two. And there was an ever changing of way of grouping subject matter and accompanying text. Charles developed an extensive grouping of nine categories – domestic architecture, interior arrangements, furniture, firegrates and mantelpieces, wall and ceiling decoration, stained glass, embroidery and textiles, pottery, porcelain, table glass and metal work, and garden furniture and garden ornaments. Geoffrey seems to have been ever fretful, trying first this and then that – so that each of his Yearbooks would prove something of a challenge to readers who had their own order of preference, and would have to flip backwards and forwards searching for their favourite topic. Sometimes he used a list like that of his father, but then decided to categorise by room as well as by object so his Yearbooks would start off with 'the exterior', 'the hall and staircase', 'the living room', 'the dining room', 'the bedroom', 'the bathroom', 'the kitchen' placed before such categories as heating and fabrics. When Rathbone and Kathleen Frost took over the editorship architecture appears to have been given pride

THE STUDIO LTD.

of place, taking up, perhaps, a disproportionate amount of the Annual, with an altogether smaller number of categories.

One issue that was sheer chaos was forgiveable, however, as it started with Geoffrey's Foreword –

Here somewhat belatedly, is the 1942/3 issue of The Studio Yearbook of Decorative Art. *There is no need to enlarge upon the difficulties that have surrounded the production of this number, they can readily be envisaged…*

the Leicester Square offices had been obliterated by bombing, with the consequential move to Chandos Place.

In hindsight *The Studio Annual of Decorative Art* can be judged as more successful than *The Studio* itself in meeting the company's original intent, for it was both definitely contemporary and international. Each new yearly issue would have been awaited eagerly by its readership as reflecting, in a stimulating way, the applied arts of the time; only, perhaps, in hindsight, can it be seen to have, indeed, been a reflection of social history, as was claimed.

Typical features in *Decorative Art*; 1940s fabric designed by Jacqueline Groag, *Alpla* aluminium kitchen by Gaby Schreiber for International Plastics Ltd., furniture by Ernest Race and 1950s *Travel* dinner service by Eric Ravilious for Wedgwood & Sons Ltd., Nils Landberg glassware for Orrefors and *Bergére* furniture suite by L. R. Ercolani for Furniture Industries Ltd.

THE KEY TO SUCCESSFUL ADVERTISING

COMMERCIAL ART has the largest circulation of any similar magazine devoted to design as a sales asset.

It is read by the leading business firms and business men who advertise, agents, printers, engravers, retailers and designers, with all of whom it has a high reputation.

It is therefore an ideal advertising medium for all engaged in publicity.

A suitably displayed announcement in its pages, costing £12 a page and pro rata, will produce unequalled results.

Apply for particulars to the Advertising Manager:
"COMMERCIAL ART," 44 LEICESTER SQ., W.C.2

COMMERCIAL ART & MODERN PUBLICITY

A full account of the birth, growth and death pangs of the journal *Commercial Art* is given in *Commercial Art, the journal that chartered 20th century commercial design*, published in 2023. In the mid-1920s The Studio Ltd. had bought a going concern, a journal titled *Commercial Art*, which had previously been launched to raise the status of commercial art (then the term used for graphic design). It was quite a step for the company to plunge into the potentially tawdry world of advertising and publicity, when, up to that time, it had largely confined its interest to 'fine' art, and the 'refined' world of architecture, interior design and furnishings. Possibly Geoffrey had had it in mind, but felt the licence to do so only after his father's death; or possibly it was on the instigation of the more commercially minded Mercer; there is no record.

The Studio Ltd. for some years kept the name *Commercial Art*; its first editorial declared its intent –

ABOVE: Poster by E. McKnight Kauffer featured in *Commercial Art*, Vol.1, 1926.
OPPOSITE: An early advertisement for *Commercial Art* designed by Kauffer.

the object is to be of service to the business man, the designer and the general public. It will show the manufacturer, retailer and advertiser what is being accomplished at home and abroad and make them familiar with the work of artists and designers

THE STUDIO LTD.

who can help them. It will place the commercial point of view before the artist, assist him to realize the needs of commerce and the conditions of mechanical reproduction. It will show the public that it is interested in beautiful things, products of everyday utility, which they can buy produced at competitive prices, and yet possess the fine, essential qualities of a work of art.

And this it set out to do, and continued to do, under the proprietorship of The Studio Ltd. for some thirty years, guided throughout by the editorship of Frank Mercer, along with, as noted, a variety of short-term co-editors, the longest-lasting being W. Gaunt. Even into the 1950s, when Rathbone is credited as editor, Mercer is still there, given as consultant editor.

Just a sample of what the first half dozen issues, published in 1926, contained, coming out in 1926, will exemplify how comprehensive its coverage was to be – printers (including Curwen, Westminster, Tolmer); products (including cars, oil, biscuits); designers (including F.C. Herrick and Maxfield Parrish); media (including press advertisements, leaflets, shop windows, posters); international examples (including Japanese posters, Hungarian labels, Viennese exhibitions); along with regular features as 'Aspects of Selling', 'New press advertising', reviews, and correspondence. Its up-to-dateness was apparent from the start, with features on film posters, the use of aerial photography, and more such.

ABOVE Advertisements from *Commercial Art* for Peugot designed by René Vincent and Standard Motor Company by Austin Cooper.
OPPOSITE A decorative design by Eckersley Lombers.

Initially *Commercial Art* focused on graphic design, aiming to raise standards, and to help give it a professional status, but into the 1930s the magazine had added photography, which was just beginning to oust graphics in advertising and publicity work. And it was in the late 1930s that the editors started to be beguiled by what was going on across the Atlantic in industrial design; so much so that the journal's title began to morph from *Commercial Art* to *Commercial Art & Industry*, to *Art & Industry*. Industrial design was, initially, to be handled somewhat clumsily, with lengthy unedited articles taking up sometimes a quarter to a third of an issue, as the editors were getting to grips with the subject matter. They wrote of the new focus –

Industrial design is a matter of increasing importance in these days of immense competition; recognized, featured and made use of to the fullest possible extent by our many competitors abroad. And every constructive effort which supplements our own activities in bringing about closer co-operation between art and industry is all to the good and will strengthen our own efforts and the interest taken in them.

Of the name change the editors wrote –

The change implies no revolutionary change of policy, but is symbolic of the place of design in industry.

ABOVE AND OPPOSITE *Art & Industry* war features; Soviet propaganda posters by Solovyev and Vyalov and R.A.A.F poster by Walter Jardine.

THE STUDIO LTD.

The Studio Ltd.'s continual internationalism – members of the AGI Conference, London, 1956; Hermann Eidenbenz, Germany, Fritz Buhler, Switzerland and Ashley Havinden, Great Britain.

The journals wartime issues contributed to morale (for there was a constant optimism to them), but, additionally, began to get people thinking about the role of design in reconstruction when war ended.

Cover of *Posters & Publicity*, The Studio Ltd.,1928.

The first and most urgent task before us is to win the war, but it is no longer out of order to consider how we shall win the peace that follows it.

Post-war, the editors filled the pages with examples of the advancement of the status of design both for reconstruction and, essentially, for rebuilding the export trade, so badly affected by the war. On *Art & Industry* celebrating its twenty fifth birthday in 1951, it was inundated with compliments from the great and the good, including Jack Beddington, formerly at Shell, Fred Phillips at the major printers, the Baynard Press , and Gordon Russell, then the Director of the Council of Industrial Design.

It was in his editorial in the issue of November 1957, that Mercer announced a change of ownership with the sell-off to the Hulton Press. He reassured the readership that no radical changes would occur; but changes there were. Rathbone's name disappeared, Mercer's was still there but a new editor, one Wilfred Walter, was to hold the reins. The title was changed, yet again, to *Design for Industry*, the pages got larger, the journal, now sub-titled 'independent international journal of industrial design', began to look like a glossy magazine. It was perhaps an overoptimistic sophisticated revamp at a time when Fleet Street was in turmoil. The December issue, in 1959, announced the journals' closure.

The editors of *Commercial Art*, under its various titles, claimed that during its lifetime it was the only industrial design magazine in Britain until the Council of Industrial Design brought out its *Design* in 1949. In its time it had helped to shift 'design' from mere ornamentation at the end of production to a more integrated role at its start; it had championed new young designers and had challenged parochialism by its international features. It became essential reading for designers and their commissioners, at the time, and remains a major source of information for those interested in the history of design in Britain in the first half of the 20th century.

As *The Studio* spawned its own annual, with its *Yearbook of Decorative Art*, so *Commercial Art* was to have, in turn, its own annual, *Modern Publicity*. Some kind of annual related to the monthly seems to have been being considered not long after *Commercial Art* had been launched. In 1924 the company published a one-off, 'Posters and their designers'. Geoffrey reported that this was so well received that it was decided to bring out a similar book the year after, and in 1925 another similar one off, *Art & Publicity* was produced. Geoffrey, with confidence, announced that there would definitely be an annual thenceforth 'illustrating the most recent developments in the association of *Art & Publicity*. In all there

ABOVE Cover of *Modern Publicity*, The Studio Ltd.,1930.

OPPOSITE Early introduction to readers of international advertising; Jyldis Tobacco by Joseph Binder, 1928 and Sools Hat Company by A. M. Cassandre, 1925.

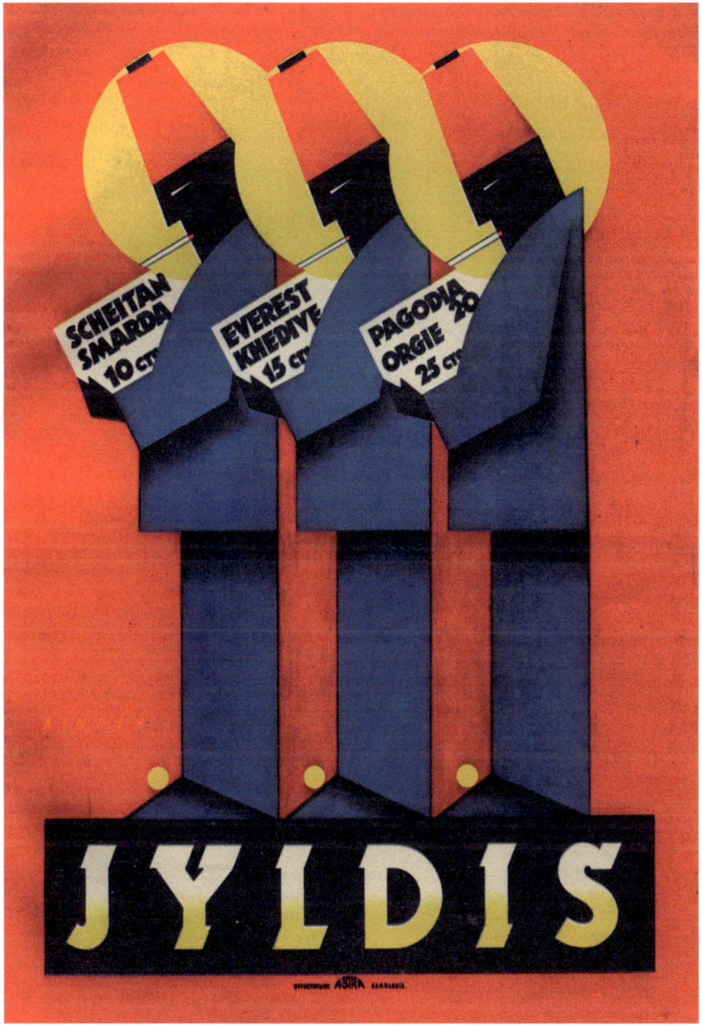
SCHEITAN
SMARDA
EVEREST
KHEDIVE
PAGODIA
ORGIE
JYLDIS

GRAND·SPORT
LA
CASQUETTE
ADOPTEE PAR
TOUS
LES CHAMPIONS
HACHARD & Cie
A.M. CASSANDRE

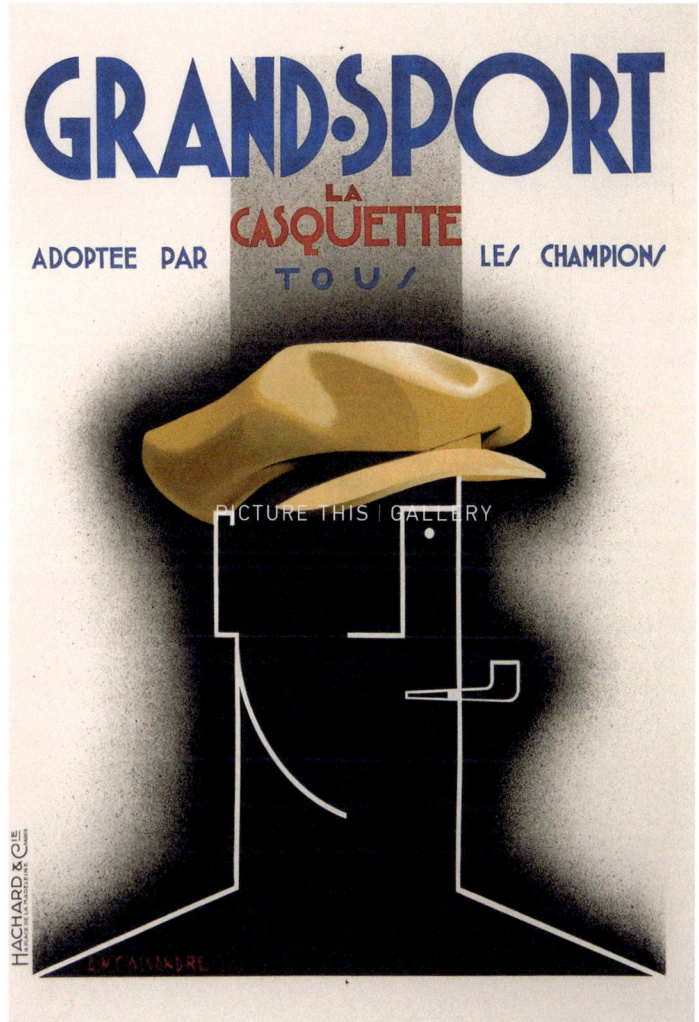

were to be six such annuals, which, in hindsight, could be described as 'trial' runs, the titles changing as Geoffrey, who edited the first few, was deciding on the possible focus. These early annuals not only established that they should encompass as broad a reflection of commercial art as possible, but that they should largely consist of illustrations with a limited text, and that examples should be international, drawn from across the world. And illustrated they were – the first, a volume of some one hundred and fifty pages, of which only eleven were text. And for many readers the foreign examples could well have been their first exposure as to what was going on in advertising and publicity in the rest of the world.

By 1930 the company had settled on the name *Modern Publicity* for these annuals, and the international characteristic of the earlier editions was clear by the first one being sectioned by country of source – England, France, Germany and America. This particular way of categorising examples of advertising and publicity material that had reached the editors haphazardly was soon abandoned, and a more systematic approach established to ensure as wide a country coverage as practical. Representatives were chosen in some twenty one countries, who were asked to put forward what they considered were 'good' examples for editorial review. The words 'international annual of advertising art', or variations of this, eventually became the annual's subtitle.

The pre-*Modern Publicity* annuals had had most of the text in a block and had tried out various criteria for grouping the illustrations, either by what was being advertised – travel, transport, food, toiletries etc. with, inevitably,

Modern Publicity, LP record cover designs, 'good' examples from 1958–59.

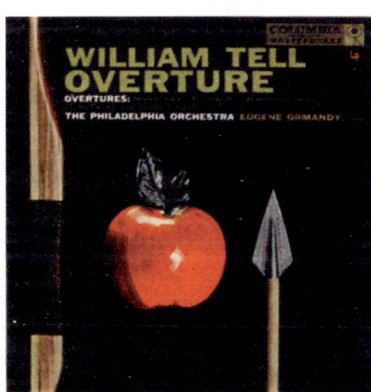
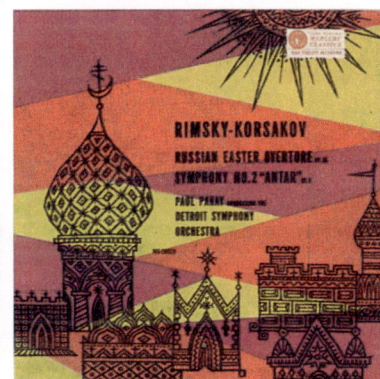

a large 'miscellaneous' section cards etc. When Mercer and Gaunt took over editorship they eventually settled on the media alternative, to which they added new sections, from time to time, such as trademarks, wine labels and record sleeves. The overall structure came to include an editorial, captioned illustrated examples, a list of advertisers, artists, agents, printers, of the illustrations, and, at the back, advertisements from companies with interests in the content – manufacturers of type, inks, paper, artist's materials and the like. And the editors, themselves, did not hold back from using *Modern Publicity* to advertise other The Studio Ltd. publications.

Early on the editors felt it necessary to put out requests for material, but as the magazine's reputation grew they began to get more contributions than they could handle. As the need to be representative was ever present the illustrations in the annual became smaller, the pages more crowded, not easily digestible. The bulk were in black and white (presumably because of the expense of colour), but occasionally, curiously, a page of examples were all printed in red, not their original colours, which made it difficult for the reader to imagine the impact of the original.

Each illustrated example was fully captioned with advertiser, designer, agency, and printer (the last so frequently overlooked but whose contribution to end result was ever crucial). When it came to British advertisements, examples from Shell and London Transport dominated in the pre-war years, setting the standard, and, indeed, Shell (in its different guises) was to be a leader throughout the life of the magazine. The key British advertising agencies most often featured were Crawfords and the London Press Exchange

Poster for restaurant Maison Prunier by A. M. Cassandre from *Modern Publicity*, 1935/36 and Roche pharmaceuticals by Levitt-Him (Lewitt-Him) from *Modern Publicity*, 1939/40.

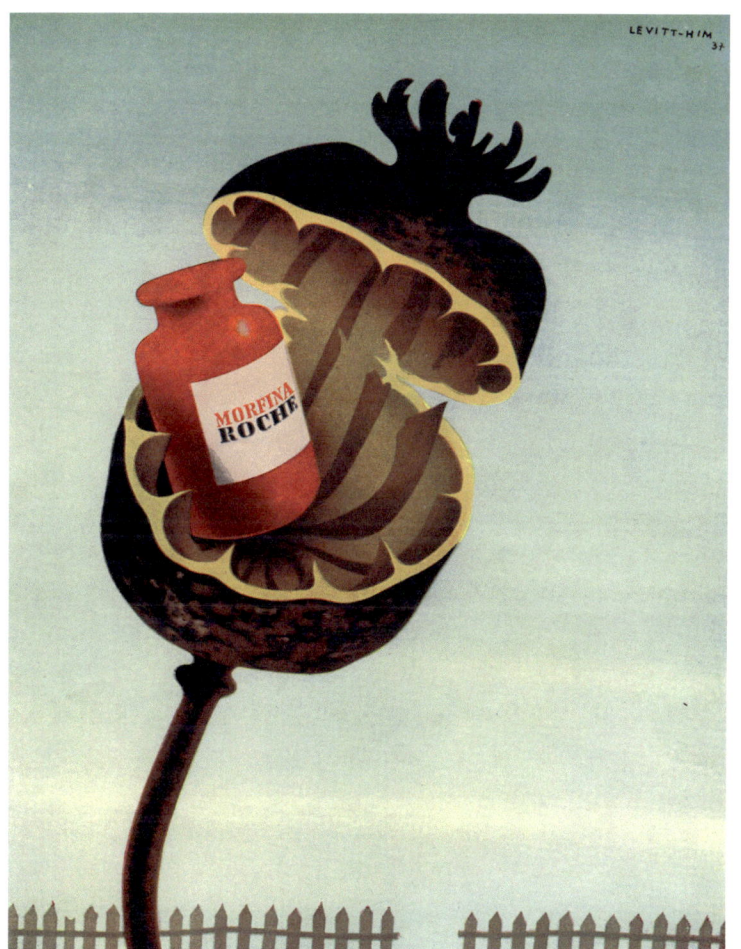

(with a later filtering in of American agencies); and for printers, the Baynard Press was the model. Of the British, or British based designers, Edward McKnight Kauffer, Gregory Brown, Austin Cooper, and Tom Purvis appeared most frequently in the pre-war issues; Hans Schleger, Abram Games, Tom Eckersley and F.H.K. Henrion in the post-war ones. And just a few examples from overseas will give a flavour of how international the magazine remained – included frequently were the French printing companies Tolmer and Draeger Frerés; the American graphic designers Joseph Binder, Paul Rand and Saul Bass, Onchi Hiroshi of Japan and the Swedish Esselte.

Although most of The Studio Ltd. monthlies and annuals included multi-cultural offerings, *Modern Publicity* was, perhaps, the one that stayed most true to Charles's original intent, for it was not only international with its named country representatives, but almost entirely visual, not laden down with text.

It was Mercer who was to edit *Modern Publicity* throughout its ownership by The Studio Ltd., as has been noted, co-edited with W. Gaunt up to the war years, and then, for brief periods, with Grace Lovat Fraser and Charles Rosner, before his continuing as editor, on his own. No slouch, Mercer was forever working not only to make *Modern Publicity* attractively readable and up-to-the-minute, but to make it influential. As editor he was a man on a mission — committed, energetic, most knowledgeable on the subject, and sensitive to the technical challenges of printing — *Modern Publicity* became a must-have, whether one was an advertiser, a designer, an agent or a printer.

Poster for Osaka Prefectural Government by Tomoichi Nishiwaki from *Modern Publicity*, 1958/59.

THE COMMERCE & INDUSTRY DEPT., OSAKA PREF. GOVT., JAPAN

OSAKA 1957

The new Studio "How to do it" Series

1. **Making an Etching**
By Levon West

2. **Wood-Engraving and Woodcuts**
By Clare Leighton

A new departure in art and craft manuals, in which the student sees the artist at work on each stage of the process, in a series of specially-taken photographs accompanied by running comment. In addition a number of works by well-known artists are illustrated with a technical commentary on each by the author. Crown 4to, special binding. *Each 7s. 6d. net.*

"... an individual who takes up one or other of these volumes should easily make himself conversant with all the necessary technicalities."—*The Scotsman.*

Other "Studio" Series

Currier & Ives Prints

1. The Spirit of America
2. The Red Indian
3. Clipper Ships

Each has eight large reproductions in colour after famous lithographs, depicting the early days in America. Royal 4to.
Each 5s. net.

Masters of Etching

29. Laura Knight, A.R.A.
30. Frank Brangwyn, R.A.
    (Second Volume)
31. C. W. R. Nevinson
32. J. McNeill Whistler
    (Second Volume)
33. Sir D. Y. Cameron, R.A. *(Second Volume)*
Each 5s. net.

Master Draughtsmen

1. Michelangelo
2. Leonardo da Vinci
3. Rubens

Each book contains 12 large reproductions and an introduction and notes upon the individual drawings. Royal 4to, boards.
Each 5s. net.

THE STUDIO LIMITED, 44 LEICESTER SQUARE, W.C.2

HOW TO DO IT & OTHER SERIES

Geoffrey, in his expansionist mode, decided to add to The Studio Ltd.'s regular publications, the category 'series' – separate books linked together by a common theme – some half dozen or so published before the 1920s were out. Of his two earliest ones, one looked back *Great Periods of Art* (including Mexican and Chinese as well as European), the next focused on contemporary *Modern Masters of Etching*. Into the 1930s, further series poured from the press covering both periods of art and groups of artists, but with the occasional oddity, as one on four leaders – political and religious – Lenin, Mustapha Kemal, Mussolini and Pius XI – actually titled *The Holme Press Series*, perhaps suggesting Geoffrey choosing subjects at will, as something crossing his path interested him. Along with 'series' on specific genre of artists (etchers, water-colourists etc.) there were such diverse topics as 'sporting prints', 'gardens and gardening' and 'new vision' with Le Corbusier writing on aircraft and Raymond Loewy on *The Locomotive!*. Also in the 'series' Geoffrey gave a nod to his father's major interest, by writing and publishing *Glimpses of Old Japan from Japanese Colour Prints*.

But it was in 1932 that the company set out, blatantly, to attract new markets, – amateurs needing technical guidance in working with arts and crafts, and, above that, the somewhat reluctant Americans. Bryan, who

Advertisement in *The Studio* announcing the *How To Do It* series December, 1932.

THIS WONDERFUL BOOK CANNOT BE REPRINTED. MAKE SURE
OF YOUR COPY NOW

MISE EN PAGE

The THEORY and PRACTICE of LAY-OUT

By A. TOLMER

A book full of ideas and experiments. Thought-provoking and stimulative. One which should be owned by everyone concerned with illustration, printing or book production.

RECEIVED WITH A CHORUS OF PRAISE AS AN EPOCH-MAKING BOOK ON ADVERTISING

Efficiency Magazine

A SUPERB BOOK OF LAY-OUT —"The Studio Ltd." has been publishing beautiful books on Commercial Art, and now it has fairly outdone itself. It has published a book on "The Theory and Practice of Lay-out"— MISE EN PAGE, by A. Tolmer. This book is an exhibition. I have never seen a book that contained as many new ideas on Commercial Art and Lay-out. It is a gold mine. . . . .

The Listener

The sparkle of French wit and dexterity pervades (the illustrations). A remarkable bargain at the price asked.

Nottingham Guardian

At first sight this extraordinary volume appears almost chaotic. The more the volume is studied the more fascinating becomes its vividly coloured pages . . . . as a printing achievement this volume has not been equalled hitherto among works of its kind.

Manchester Guardian

The book is full of suggestions. We must once more express our indebtedness to "The Studio" publications for an excellent production.

W. D. H. McCullough

A most exciting volume . . . . To the advertiser . . . . an educational hand book. We prophesy a very long run for this production. Every page is a typographical adventure.

John o' London's Weekly

. . . perhaps the most unexpected and breath-taking book yet published. It is obviously meant as a book of examples and suggestions, and so used will be of great service to the artist and lay-out man.

The British Printer

The "lay-out" is discussed with a veritable wealth of examples, most of which are luxurious specimens of printing, and the essentials of good lay-out are driven home logically.

MEDIUM QUARTO. IN HANDSOME BINDING 30s. NET

The Studio Ltd., 44 Leicester Square, London

'HOW TO DO IT' & OTHER SERIES

was being tasked with developing a market from the New York office, described his challenge – 'Times were hard, there were breadlines on Fourth Avenue'; what the company was publishing at the time neither suited the American purse nor its taste. With records extant, the precise origins of the *How to do it* series' is unknown, but Bryan wrote of it 'saving the day'.

ABOVE *Magazine Illustration*, *How To Do It* 78, The Studio Ltd., 1959.
OPPOSITE Advertisement for *Mise en Page*, The Studio, 1931.

…to tell step by step, how to paint, draw, sculpt, photograph, make pottery etc. We told ourselves that the only excuse for being so 'commercial' as to publish technical books was to make our 'How to's' more glamorous than those on any other publisher's list. This was achieved by the rather clever idea of varnishing the large half-tone plates and tipping them on to blank pages facing text. Both aesthetically and commercially, the experiment worked beautifully.

The original *How to do it* series consisted of just under eighty books; but there were to be additional related series, including; *Hours of Leisure* and, throughout the Second World War, *How to Draw* and *Make it yourself*.

To appeal to the American market US based authors were sought, along with British ones, but most, whichever side of the Atlantic they

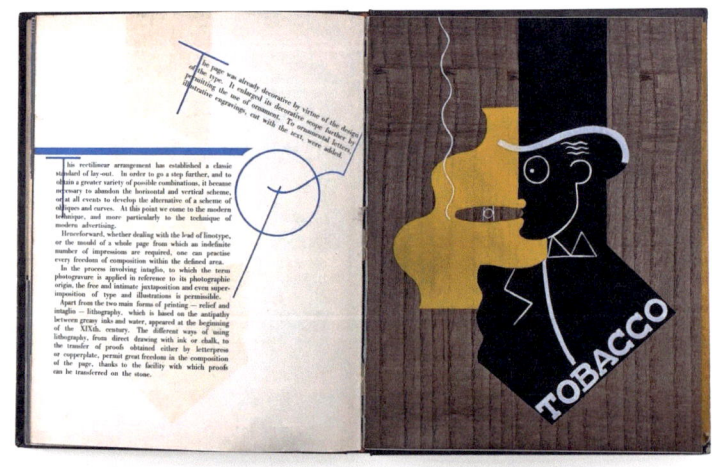
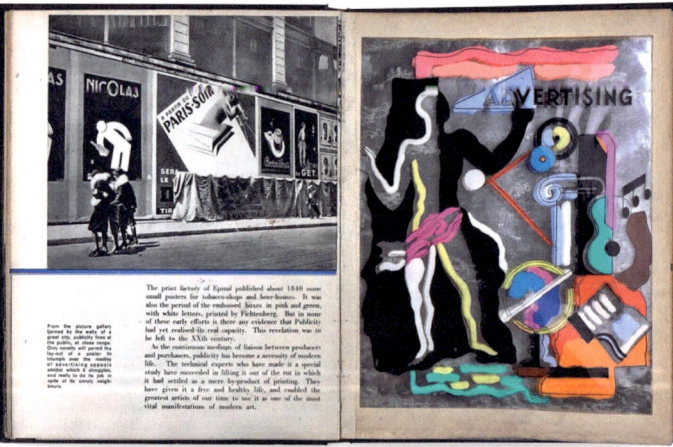
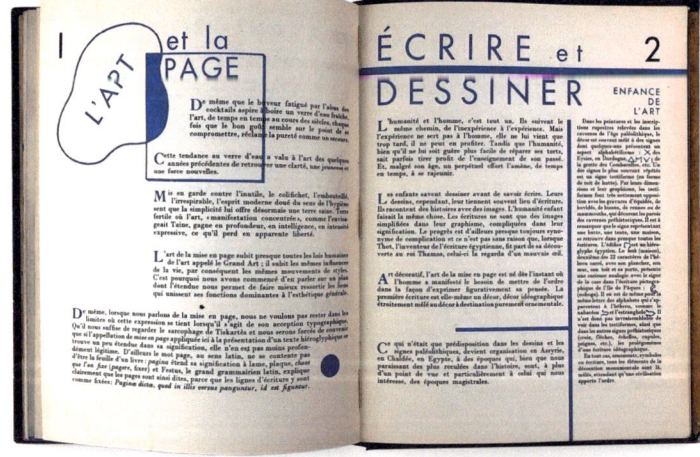

came from, are now long forgotten. However, in hindsight, a few of the British ones were to build considerable reputations for themselves, as Clare Leighton who provided a *How to do it* on wood cuts, Ashley Havinden on line drawing, Duncan Miller on interior decorating, Francis Marshall on fashion design, Doris Zinkeisen on designing for the stage, Tom Eckersley on poster design, Milner Gray on package design, Terence Conran on textile design and Terence Cuneo on drawing tanks!

The Studio Ltd. published some twenty series in all. Most were relatively short-lived, but the *How to do it* one was a survivor, to continue for over twenty five years, saving the company's American office, and, no doubt, subsidizing some of the more esoteric series published from its London base

ABOVE *Less*, GPO poster 1945, Tom Eckersley, from *Poster Design*, *How To Do It* 50, The Studio Ltd., 1954. OPPOSITE *Mise En Page: The Theory And Practice Of Lay-Out*, The Studio, 1931.

We have MOVED

*

The new address of
THE STUDIO LTD
and all its publications, including

THE STUDIO
ART & INDUSTRY
DECORATIVE ART
MODERN PUBLICITY

is

HULTON HOUSE
Fleet Street, London, E.C.4

EPILOGUE

The Studio Ltd., existing for over fifty years, was a pioneer in the publishing world on a number of fronts. It was one of the first British publishers to specialise in the arts, certainly the first to publish both magazines *and* books on the subject. And, in doing that, the company was at the forefront of bringing the arts of the world to the notice of its readership, its internationalism seeping through its monthly, annual, series, and special publications.

Further, it was a crusader for standards and professional status for commercial art and for industrial design, gaining them the respect that had previously been reserved for 'fine' art and craftsmanship. And from its specials to its *How to do it series*, it was to appeal to a wide readership, from academics to amateurs, from researchers to constructors in their garden sheds or walkers carrying sketchbook and pencil.

And all of this achieved largely by amateurs – 'amateur' in the best sense of the word, doing something for the sheer love of it. None of the Holmes had any kind of professional or technical training. Charles was motivated both by social idealism and aesthetic passions, Geoffrey by his personal enthusiasms, Rathbone and Bryan by aesthetic interest and pride in inheritance. Profit, market dominance, and other such materialistic motives, if they existed in the Holmes at all, were down the pecking order to sentiment.

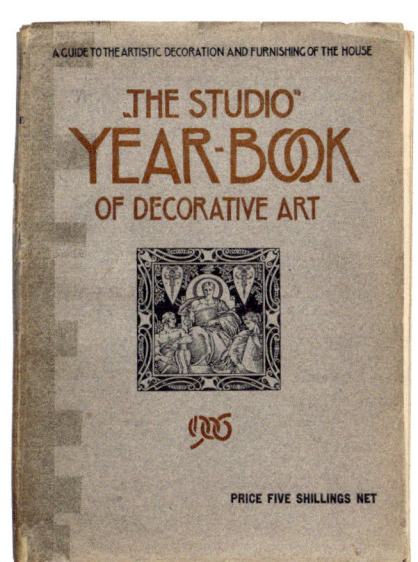

ABOVE Cover of the first *Studio Year Book*, 1906.
OPPOSITE Hulton Press takeover, *Modern Publicity* 1957–58.

EPILOGUE

It is, perhaps paradoxical, that *The Studio* magazine, the publication giving the company its name, and best remembered when the company is mentioned (sometimes the only publication thought to have been published by the company) was, perhaps, the least satisfactory. Possibly from a desire to be even-handed in what was offered to its readership, possibly from the aesthetic tastes of family members, The Studio Ltd. in the area of 'fine' art, tended to avoid the controversial, the radical; its readers would have found plenty that was 'pleasant', but altogether less that would have set their hearts on fire or influenced the course of their lives, that some of The Studio Ltd.'s other publications could well have done. Yet it was *The Studio*, of the two monthlies and two annuals, that was to survive the longest.

After the death of Geoffrey Holme the publications were sold on, and on, and on again – from one short-lived optimistic publisher to the next; from the Hulton Press, to the Longacre Press, to Cory, Adams and Mackay through to the National Magazine Co. But with such dedicated editors as G.S. Whittet, Peter Townsend (and his contemporary art enthusiastic assistants), and Richard Cork, along with such confident designers as David Pelham, who was later to become Art Director of Penguin Books, the somewhat staid *The Studio* of the Holmes was to morph into a truly sophisticated, international journal of contemporary art.

Nevertheless when Sims Reed, in 1978, provided a listing of what The Studio Ltd. had published over the years, it neatly summed up what the Holme's family *had* achieved –

A selection of covers, 1961–63, designed by David Pelham.

EPILOGUE

In retrospect, the magazines and books… represent one of the most complete documents on the history of ideas of late nineteenth and twentieth century art. Nowhere else can one find such detailed reference not only to the major artists and designers, but also to the more minor figures.

A unique family affair!

The Three Men of Gotham, design for a printed velvet by C. F. A. Voysey, c.1889, illustrated in first issue of *The Studio*, 1893.

EDUCATIONAL.

ST. JOHN'S WOOD ART SCHOOLS
7 ELM TREE ROAD, N.W.

Honorary Advisory Council:
Sir LAWRENCE ALMA-TADEMA, O.M., R.A.
J. W. WATERHOUSE, Esq., R.A.
G. CLAUSEN, Esq., R.A.
and other Members of the Royal Academy.

Principals:
FREDERICK D. WALENN
LEONARD WALKER, R.B.A.
A. MICHAELSON, R.B.A.
PICKERING WALKER

Painting and Drawing from Elementary to Advanced Life-work

Students may enter at any time

Great success has been achieved in preparing Students for the Royal Academy Schools. During the year ending in July last twenty-five students have been passed in on probation.

THE POLYTECHNIC SCHOOL OF ART, REGENT ST.
Headmaster: G. P. GASKELL, R.B.A., R.E.
DAY & EVENING CLASSES IN DRAWING, PAINTING, MODELLING & DESIGN

LIFE CLASSES (Figure and Costume), for Men and Women, are held every day and every evening (except Saturday)
MODELLING LIFE CLASS, five times weekly
Classes in DESIGN, FIGURE COMPOSITION, DRAWING FOR REPRODUCTIONS, etc., every day and every evening

In the National Competitions of the last six years this School obtained a higher aggregate of awards than any other London Art School

The School re-opened with greatly extended premises in the New Building in Sept. last

Prospectus on application to the Director of Education, The Polytechnic, 307-311 Regent Street, W.

HERBERT E. BUTLER
Gives instruction in Painting (Oil and Watercolour), Figure and Landscape, at
POLPERRO, CORNWALL.

Large and convenient Modern Studio with glasshouse annexe for study from the Model in outdoor effect. Mrs. Butler receives Pupils as Paying Guests. Ideal situation. All modern conveniences. Special terms for resident pupils. For particulars apply to HERBERT E. BUTLER, The Orchard, Polperro, Cornwall.

A PIONEERING PRINTER

LUND HUMPHRIES OF BRADFORD

The **FULLY ILLUSTRATED** book by **RUTH ARTMONSKY**, Author

Available from ACC ART BOOKS
(accartbooks.com)

KAUFFER'S COVERS

The Book Jackets and Covers of Edward McKnight Kauffer

This book by **RUTH ARTMONSKY** & **BRIAN WEBB**

is the first on this aspect of his work, includes illustrations of some **250 JACKETS** and an account of the publishers who commissioned them.

Available from ALL GOOD BOOKSHOPS

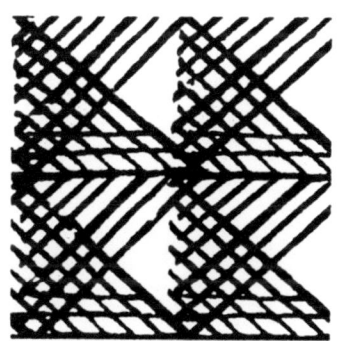

ENID MARX

Design

BOOKS BY RUTH ARTMONSKY

JACK BEDDINGTON, A FOOTNOTE MAN, 2006; The School Prints, 2006; Art for Everyone, 2007; A Snapper up of Unconsidered Trifles, 2008; Bringers of Good Tidings, 2009; Shipboard Style, 2010; 'Do you want it good or do you want it Tuesday?', 2011; Designing Women, 2012; The Pleasures of Printing, 2013; Showing Off, 2013; Exhibiting Ourselves, 2014; **BILL CRAWFORD, MOVING THE HEARTS AND MINDS OF MEN**, 2014; Unashamed Artists, 2014; Art for the Ear, 2015; Here's to Your Health, (with Stella Harpley), 2015; Tom Purvis: Art for the Sake of Money, 2015; **THE BEST ADVERTISING COURSE IN TOWN**, 2015; Powering the Home, 2016; **FROM PALACES TO PRE-FABS**, 2017; The Golden Age of British Advertising, 2018; **WRAPPING IT UP**, 2019; Advertising Modernism, 2020; **CRUSADERS OF ART AND DESIGN 1920-1970**, 2020; Sellers of Dreams 1920-1970, 2020; **KAUFFER'S COVERS**, 2021; **A PIONEERING PRINTER: LUND HUMPHRIES OF BRADFORD**, 2022; Becoming a Designer, 2022; Commercial Art, 2023; Printing People, 2023; **HENRIETTA STREET**, 2023; London press exchange, 2024.

THE LONDON & NEW ART SCHOOL

STRATFORD STUDIOS, KENSINGTON, W.

DRAWING, PAINTING, COMPOSITION, ILLUSTRATION, POSTER DESIGN, ANATOMY

Teaching Staff:
PHILLIP A. LASZLÓ, M.V.O. HON. R.B.A.

RICHARD JACK   C. M. Q. ORCHARDSON, R.O.I.
JOHN HASSALL, R.I.   EDMUND J. SULLIVAN, A.R.W.S.
FRANCKLYN HELMORE   MISS U. W. A. PARKES

STUDENTS MAY JOIN AT ANY TIME

Further particulars on application to the Secretary:
Mrs. HELMORE, Stratford Studios, Stratford Road, Kensington, W.

TEL.—KENSINGTON 3065

S. Martin's School of Art

3 Castle St., Endell St., Long Acre, W.C.
Principal: JOHN E. ALLEN, A.R.C.A.

DAY AND EVENING CLASSES for Drawing, Painting, Designing, Modelling, and Art Needlework.
LIFE CLASS (Day)—*Costume and Figure*: Tuesday, Wednesday, Thursday, Friday, Saturday, 10 to 4.
  ,, ,, (Evening)—*Figure*: Monday, Wednesday and Friday.
             Costume: Tuesday and Thursday.
LADIES' FIGURE CLASS—Wednesdays, 10 to 4.

FASHION

Sketching and Designing in line, wash, chalk and colour. Also Black-and-White Book and Story Illustrating, Poster and Showcard Designing. Lessons at Studios or by Post

Students' Drawings placed, Good positions found.
Terms, Secretary: A. SEYMOUR.
The Commercial Art Reproduction Training School,
'Phone: GERRARD 2278   **114 NEW OXFORD STREET, W.C.**

LAMBETH SCHOOL OF ART

St. Oswald's Place, Upper Kennington Lane, S.E.

LIFE SCHOOL
DAY AND EVENING CLASSES

THOMAS McKEGGIE, A.R.C.A., Principal

Life Classes for Women.	Life Classes for Men.
Head . . Mon., Wed. & Friday.	Head . . Mon., Wed. & Friday.
Costume Model Mon., Wed. & Friday.	Costume Model Mon., Wed. & Friday.
Full-length Figure Tuesday & Thursday.	Full-length Figure Mon., Wed. & Friday.

Figure Composition, Book Decoration and Illustration, "Black-and-White" Drawing for Reproduction, Landscape, Still Life, Flower Painting, Miniature Painting, Modelling, and all the usual Preparatory Classes. Junior and Senior Sketch Clubs.

PROSPECTUS ON APPLICATION